Laugh, Clown, Cry

The Story of Charlie Chaplin

By Walter Oleksy

 **RAINTREE EDITIONS**

Printed in the United States of America.

1 2 3 4 5 6 7 8 9 0   80 79 78 77 76

Library of Congress Number: 76-15001

Published by 🌲 Raintree Editions
                   A Division of Raintree Publishers Limited
                   Milwaukee, Wisconsin 53203

Distributed by   Childrens Press
                      1224 West Van Buren Street
                      Chicago, Illinois 60607

Library of Congress Cataloging in Publication Data

Oleksy, Walter G 1930-
    Laugh, clown, cry: the story of Charlie Chaplin.

    SUMMARY: A biography of Charlie Chaplin which
reveals his attitudes, successes, and failures.
Illustrated with black and white photographs.
    1. Chaplin, Charles, 1889-   —Juvenile literature.
[1. Chaplin, Charles, 1889-   2. Actors and
actresses]   I. Title.
PN2287.C504   791.43'028'0924 [B]   [92]   76-15001
ISBN 0-8172-0427-X
ISBN 0-8172-0426-1 lib. bdg

Contents

Charlie Chaplin in his classic Tramp costume.

Introduction

The movie being shot was supposed to be a comedy. But the star, Ford Sterling, a tall and beefy man with a small black beard, just wasn't being funny.

The producer, Mack Sennett, munched nervously on his cigar and fidgeted while expensive film was being hand-cranked through the cameras. Suddenly desperate, he turned to a young comedian beside him, whom he had just hired a few days before.

"Get in there and do something funny!" Sennett ordered.

The young actor, dark haired and rather frail looking, saw the situation and knew he had to do something fast. But how could he be funny on a moment's notice?

He needed something to wear. That much he knew. He couldn't be funny in the somber business suit he was wearing.

He ran off the set to a wardrobe room and rummaged through piles of old clothes. Finally he found a few things . . . some baggy pants, shoes too big for him, a frock coat too small, and a derby hat. All in black.

He put on the clothes, but still hadn't any idea how he was going to be funny in them. Rushing back to the set—a hotel lobby—he put on a small, black, square-shaped mustache, to make him look older. Before he reached the set, he picked up a bamboo cane to take along.

He was all dressed now. But he still didn't know who he was in the outfit, or how to be funny.

Suddenly he felt like strutting. It seemed to him that the clothes were taking over his personality. He began acting like a man who is down and out, but who refuses to admit it.

The producer growled: "What on earth do you intend doing in those rags?"

"I'm a tramp," the actor replied. "But not just *any* tramp. I'm a many-sided tramp. A gentleman, a poet, a dancer, a dreamer. A lonely fellow, always hopeful of romance and adventure. Maybe even fortune."

"All right," Sennett said, not too sure. "Get on that set and do something funny!"

The Tramp entered the hotel lobby and immediately tripped over the leg of a lady seated in a stuffed chair. He turned and politely raised his derby to her, to apologize.

Then he turned again and tripped over an umbrella stand. Getting up, he raised his hat to the umbrella stand.

The producer and everyone on the set began to laugh. It was simple, but very funny. Their laughter wouldn't spoil the scene, because this was a silent picture, back in 1914 before sound came to the movies.

After that one scene, a new star was born. He was Charlie Chaplin, and the Tramp he played became the most famous character ever created by a comedian.

He was "the little fellow," a pathetic and lovable little man with a funny mustache. He walked like a penguin, and he twirled his cane no matter how down on his luck he might be.

Chaplin had a genius for making people laugh. But he also made them cry. His comedy touched a note of truth in people that made them understand themselves and their fellow man better.

Chaplin was perhaps the funniest person in the world. Perhaps he also was one of the unhappiest. He was independent, a loner most of his life. He was a genius, and few people understand geniuses.

After more than a quarter century as the world's favorite comedian, Chaplin suddenly became one of America's most disliked men. Speeches he made before America entered World War II were misunderstood.

Chaplin had tried to raise money for starving Russians when Germany invaded their country. Because of his speeches, many Americans decided that he must be a Communist.

Actually, Chaplin was simply for everyone's freedom, and for helping those who needed help, no matter what their country's politics. But a nation's love for him turned to hatred almost overnight. He couldn't understand why people suddenly stopped going to see his movies, no longer laughed at him, and even wanted him thrown out of the country.

When he sailed for England to show his wife and small children the country where he was born, he got a cable aboard ship. It told him he wasn't welcome to return to America. He was a person not wanted.

It would be 20 years before he would be forgiven for something he never did.

Early Days

Charlie Chaplin was born on April 16, 1889, in an old three-story brick building in an unfashionable middle-class neighborhood in London. His father, Charles Chaplin, was of French and Irish descent. Mr. Chaplin was a short, chunky man with brooding, dark eyes. He had a light baritone voice and was quite successful in vaudeville.

Chaplin's mother, Hannah, was very pretty, and dainty and charming. Her father was Irish, but she had a bit of gypsy in her on her mother's side of the family. For all his life, Charlie Chaplin would love his mother, and be proud of his romantic gypsy heritage.

Hannah also sang professionally in music halls. She met Charles Chaplin when they were in a play together. She was 16 then, and playing the lead. They became sweethearts.

But when Hannah was 18, she impulsively eloped to Africa with a man who was older and very rich. She soon decided that it had been a mistake. After a little more than a year of luxurious living in Africa, she left the man and returned to England. She brought her infant son, Sydney.

In London, she and Chaplin fell in love again and were married. But Hannah Chaplin hadn't been aware of a major flaw in the handsome actor-singer she had married. He was a heavy drinker, and he soon became an alcoholic. Four years after their marriage, Hannah separated from him—shortly after Charlie was born.

Hannah Chaplin kept singing to earn a living for herself and her two children. But she started to have trouble with her voice. After a while, she earned very little and the family moved a lot—usually without paying the rent. Charlie's father never came to see them and rarely sent them any money.

When Charlie was little, he was standing in the wings of a London music hall where his mother was singing on stage. He heard her voice crack. So did the audience. They began to laugh at her. The stage manager acted quickly. He grabbed Charlie by the hand and led him toward the stage.

Charlie went out before the footlights and began singing. The audience loved him. They began tossing coins onto the stage. Charlie stopped singing. He told the audience that he would pick up the money first and sing afterward.

His speech brought laughter and more coins. The stage manager came out to help Charlie pick up the coins. But Charlie looked like he didn't trust the stage manager, and this made the audience laugh even more.

That was Charlie's first appearance before an audience, and his mother's last. Illnesses brought on by worry and poverty had ruined her voice, which had never been strong. She had to give up the stage and, after a while, turned to sewing and dressmaking. But she didn't make much money, and the family fell into deeper poverty.

Finally they moved into a one-room basement apartment. While Hannah sewed, Sydney took odd jobs selling papers, running errands, or sweeping floors. But there was never enough income.

Soon Hannah fell behind in the payments on her sewing machine, and the creditors took it from her. When she couldn't find any other work, she grew desperate and sick. There was only one course left for her, and she took it. She packed their few belongings and took her sons to the Lambeth Workhouse.

Workhouses were places where the poor both lived and worked. They earned very little, but at least had a roof over their heads and something to eat. Often it was the last step a person took before becoming a charity case.

For Hannah, turning herself and her sons over to a workhouse was especially humiliating. Once she had been a woman of wealth; mistress of a fine home in Africa. Even as a music hall singer, she had earned enough money to keep her family and her self-respect. Now she had lost even that.

It was hard for Charlie and Sydney, too. It hadn't occurred to them that when they entered the workhouse, they would be separated from their mother. Hannah was taken to the women's ward and the boys were taken to the children's ward. There they lived with other unfortunate boys.

What shocked Charlie most—even more than having all his hair shaved off for reasons of cleanliness—was his first visit with his mother. They had been apart for only a short time. But how she had aged! Pale and embarrassed, and wearing an old work dress, Hannah sat with her two boys on a hard bench in a visiting room. They embraced each other and wept.

Hannah tried to cheer them up, and out of her apron pocket she gave them some coconut candy. She told them she bought the candy with a little money she had left from doing some hand-sewing for one of the nurses at the workhouse. She told Charlie and Sydney not to worry—their hair would grow back soon. And somehow they would find a way to get out of the workhouse and be together again.

Not long afterward, Charlie and Sydney were taken from Lambeth to the Hanwell School for Orphans and Destitute Children. A horse-drawn van took Charlie and Sydney 12 miles out of London to the country and the Hanwell School. About 400 boys and girls lived at Hanwell. Some had parents who were too poor to keep them, some came from broken homes, and some had no parents at all.

Charlie and Sydney were getting used to adjusting to any situation, and found that they could survive in the school for destitute children. But Charlie found the nights hard to bear. He missed his mother. And he worried about her, alone at Lambeth Workhouse.

Charlie and Sydney lived at Hanwell for a little more than a year. It was not the easiest year of their lives. Once, a ringworm epidemic swept through the school. Boys and girls infected were forced to have all their hair shaved off and their heads stained with iodine. Once again Charlie lost his dark curly locks.

The only bright spot in all this gloom was a visit from his mother. She had regained some of her health, and Charlie hoped that the family might be reunited.

Soon afterward, Charlie's dream came true. His mother was allowed to leave the workhouse. She had enough money to rent a room near a park for herself and the boys. But once again, she had trouble finding work and supporting the family. So they ended up back in the workhouse.

A short time later, the boys were sent word that their mother had gone insane and had been committed to a lunatic asylum. Sydney cried, but not Charlie. A strange, vague despair fell over Charlie. He felt as if none of it were real.

Authorities decided to place the boys in the care of their father. Charlie found himself excited about the prospect that they would be living together. Charlie had seen his father only twice in all his life. Once he had seen him on the stage, and another time his father had walked past their house with a lady.

The boys were brought from the workhouse to a small house with a garden in London. This was where their father lived, but he was not at home. A lady met them at the door. An infant boy was playing on the parlor floor. Without her telling them, they knew that the child was their half brother.

When their father came home that night, he was kind to them. But, all in all, their life together was strained. The woman, Louise, immediately had a falling-out with Sydney over where he would sleep, and took every opportunity to complain about him to their father. Because Sydney was unhappy, Charlie was, too.

The boys were enrolled in a school nearby, and a life of sorts began for them in the home of their father. Louise, however, turned out to be as heavy a drinker as their father. More often than not, she took out her frustrations on Sydney. By now Charlie was 8 years old, and Sydney was 12. Charlie was too young to escape the unhappy home when things got really bad, but Sydney stayed out late to be away from their foster mother.

Late one night, Louise began to argue with Sydney, and ripped the bedclothes off him. She had been drinking. It was the last straw for Sydney. He threatened to poke her with a buttonhook he had sharpened to a point if she tried to hit him. That was the beginning of the end for Charlie and Sydney's stay with their father.

Fortunately, Hannah had recovered her health and was released from the asylum. Sydney and Charlie shared their mother's joy that they would be together again, even if they would be living crowded in one room.

While his mother worked as a seamstress, Charlie went to school. He was not interested in school subjects, but school plays appealed to him. And he was good at reciting and acting. He was disappointed when there was no part for him in the school's Christmas show, *Cinderella*. He wanted to play one of the ugly sisters!

Sydney eventually got a job as a bugler on a passenger boat, and their father arranged for Charlie to get started in his stage career. Charlie became one of the Eight Lancashire Lads, an act of child clog dancers.

Charlie was not an especially good dancer, but he would take any opportunity that would get him into show business. More important, he felt proud to bring some money home to his mother.

Early in his career with the Eight Lancashire Lads, Charlie wanted to be funny in front of an audience. He managed to talk one of the other boy dancers into teaming with him as "Bristol and Chaplin, the Millionaire Tramps." Even at that early age, he began experimenting with the Tramp that later would become his trademark.

But audiences preferred the Eight Lancashire Lads' dancing, and Charlie and his young friend Bristol never did get to perform their tramp act before an audience.

Charlie and the other Lancashire boys got jobs playing cats and dogs in a show at the London Hippodrome. Charlie played a cat, wearing a mask and black tights. But Charlie's career with the Eight Lancashire Lads ended shortly after this engagement. His mother felt he looked sickly. He was sent home, and soon after developed asthma. Without his income, the family again fell on hard times.

Things got a little better when Sydney came home on leave. He brought home a lot of money he had saved, and told stories of his adventures at sea. It was a good time for the family—their "cake-and-ice-cream period." But soon after Sydney went back to his job, Hannah's health began to deteriorate. She seldom could find work, and Charlie was still too young to earn enough for them both to live on. Before long, Hannah was again sent to an asylum, and Charlie was on his own.

Footlights

Charlie got his first real stage part when he was 12. He played a pageboy in *Sherlock Holmes*. London critics and audiences noticed and liked him. Charlie went on tour with the play to other cities in England. Eventually he got Sydney a small part in *Sherlock Holmes*, too, and the brothers toured together.

After *Sherlock Holmes* ended its run, Sydney joined Fred Karno's Company, a troupe of traveling comedians. Charlie went to work for Casey's Circus, a vaudeville act. Charlie and some other young boys and girls played grownups in different characters in stories and history. Charlie gained valuable experience as a comedian.

Although he missed his mother and brother, Charlie loved working and living with show people. He lived in boarding houses that catered to actors and singers, jugglers and musicians, acrobats and magicians. Charlie enjoyed talking with them, watching them practice, and eating with them family-style at big boarding house tables. He had virtually lost his own family; show people became like a new family to him.

Charlie was 17 now, still not tall, but rather good looking. His dark, curly hair had straightened out a little, and he wore it parted in the middle, which was the fashion in 1906. He looked both bright and sensitive, but he could quickly change his appearance to fit most any character he was asked to play.

After a week's work as the juvenile lead in a dull play called *The Merry Major,* Charlie tried his hand at writing. (In later years, Charlie would become one of the few performers who wrote, directed, and produced his own movies, and even wrote all the music for them.)

Charlie wrote a slapstick comedy sketch which he sold to a vaudeville hypnotist. Charlie was to direct the playlet. But a few days later, during rehearsals, the hypnotist changed his mind about producing the sketch.

Shortly after this disappointment, Sydney's boss sent for Charlie. Fred Karno was a successful producer who had several music hall shows going in London and in other cities. In earlier days, Karno had been an acrobat and comedian. He told Charlie that he needed a comedian to replace one who wasn't very funny.

Charlie told Karno that all he needed was the chance. He knew he could be funny.

Karno liked Charlie's confidence in himself and signed him on with one of his London music hall troupes for a two-week trial engagement. If Charlie made good with the audiences, he would get a year's contract.

His first test was to warm up the audience for the leading comedian, Harry Weldon, in a sketch called *The Football Match.* This was a slapstick affair about football players in a locker room.

The show opened at a big music hall, the London Coliseum. Charlie was a bundle of nerves. The orchestra began playing a rousing song, the curtain went up, and the audience watched a dozen football players exercising. After a few minutes, the players ran off into the wings—supposedly going to the playing field—leaving an empty stage.

This was Charlie's cue. His mind suddenly cleared as he walked onstage and stood alone. His back was to the audience. He was dressed to look like an older man, in a long black coat, top hat, cane, and white spats over his shoes. He was playing a well-dressed villain.

When Charlie turned around and showed his fake red nose to the audience, he got some laughs. That helped him relax, and he went into character, acting the villain. He crossed the stage and he tripped over a dumbbell. The audience laughed at that, too. Then his cane got tangled up in a punching bag. The bag swung out and came back, hitting him in the face. Charlie staggered and spun around, hitting himself in the head with his cane. The audience howled with laughter and delight.

While the laughs came faster, Charlie suddenly felt his pants falling down. He had lost a button and nothing was holding them up. Instead of panicking, Charlie pretended it was all part of the show.

Charlie walked slowly off the stage then, his small part of warming up the audience finished. He had done a good job. Weldon had no trouble getting laughs.

After the show, Weldon grudgingly told Charlie he was all right. And Karno was delighted.

Charlie as he looked when he toured England with Fred Karno's Company.

The next day, Charlie sent Sydney a telegram with the good news. Karno had signed him to a year's contract at about $25 a week, more money than Charlie had ever earned before. The thought of having a contract guaranteeing him that much money every week for a year was enough to make him celebrate.

When the show finished its London run about three and a half months later, Charlie and the company toured England. After the year was up, both Charlie and Sydney were back in London and took a small apartment together.

With such success, it was inevitable that Charlie would now fall in love. The girl was a dancer named Hetty Kelly, one of Bert Coutts' Yankee Doodle Girls. This show ran on the same bill with one Charlie was in for Fred Karno. She asked Charlie to hold a mirror for her so she could check her hair before going onstage. Charlie thought he had never seen a girl as beautiful as Hetty.

After only a few brief dates, Charlie asked Hetty if she would marry him. It was too sudden for Hetty, who was only 17, and she turned him down. The broken romance affected Charlie for a very long time.

Charlie's contract with Karno was renewed for the next two years. The constant work as a comedian helped Charlie polish the many character parts he would later use to even greater success. Karno sent Charlie to Paris with one of his shows. Charlie was 20 years old. Audiences who couldn't even understand English laughed at the antics of Charlie and the rest of the troupe. They performed mainly in pantomime because of the language barrier. Acting in pantomime—doing funny things without saying anything at all— became second nature to Charlie. This also helped him develop skills he would put to use in silent films.

After his success in Paris, Karno sent Charlie and the troupe to America. Charlie was to headline the show as star comedian.

In 1910, Charlie arrived by ship in New York. But American audiences didn't care much for the show. They could hardly understand the British accents.

One critic, however, noticed Charlie: "There was at least one funny Englishman in the troupe and he will do for America."

After the show closed in New York, the company toured the United States for almost six months. They traveled all the way to California before returning to New York. Although the company expected to return to England, they got a six-week job in New York with a show called *A Night in an English Music Hall*. It was much more popular than the original show.

Among those who howled at Charlie's performance was Mack Sennett. He was then working as an extra for D. W. Griffith, master of silent films.

After watching Charlie in the show, Sennett told a friend that if he ever got into the movie business, he'd sign up Charlie.

The company again was signed for a 20-week tour of the US. At the end of the tour, Charlie looked forward to returning to England.

He found Sydney married. His mother was quite ill and confined to a room at the asylum. Charlie was depressed. The family he looked forward to returning to was gone. He was home-less. He decided to return to the United States as soon as possible.

After four months' work in England, Charlie returned to the United States with Fred Karno's Company. They played New York and again went on tour.

While touring with the show in Philadelphia, Charlie got a telegram. It was from two motion picture producers, part owners of the Keystone Company. Mack Sennett had left Griffith, formed his own movie-making company—the Keystone Company—and wanted Charlie to work for him.

The Keystone comedies specialized in slap-stick. Charlie was not too happy about that. But Keystone offered Charlie a one-year contract at $150 a week. It was a small fortune to Charlie; more money than he had ever dreamed of earn-ing. And working with Keystone meant a lot of publicity. When his contract was up, Charlie planned to return to vaudeville as an internation-al star.

But the turning point in Charlie's life really came a few months later, when Sennett sent him out onto a set to do something funny.

Sennett told Charlie that they needed some gags, and asked Charlie to get together some comedy makeup. Charlie went to the wardrobe section, and within a very short time the Tramp was born.

As the Tramp, Charlie probably was the fun-niest comedian in the movies. But more than that, he changed the whole basis of movie comedy. At first, his directors tried to force Charlie into making people laugh the way all the other comedians did it: a pie in the face, a pratfall into a puddle of mud, an auto chase. Charlie got into trouble with his directors over his suggestions for different kinds of gags. Soon he was known as difficult to work with.

But after a while, Charlie won the right to write, direct, and star in his own films. His Tramp got into and out of situations the average moviegoer could identify with. Along with their laughter, Charlie drew their tears.

Charlie recommended his brother Sydney to Sennett. Sennett was anxious to hire another Chaplin. So Sydney and his wife came to Hollywood to work for Keystone. But Sydney soon gave up acting to manage Charlie's fast-growing career.

In 1914, his first year in Hollywood, Charlie made 34 short comedies. Even in those early days of silent movies when Hollywood was a series of factories churning out movies every few days, making 34 films in one year was a heavy load. For so many of the movies to be as good as they were was even more amazing.

Portrait of Chaplin in 1914.

Derby Days

In his first movie, *Making a Living*, Charlie wore a black coat, top hat, monocle, and drooping mustache. He is penniless, but pretends to be a wealthy nobleman. To win the heart of a newspaper publisher's daughter, Charlie outwits a photographer, beats him in a chase, and scoops his rival by turning in much-wanted news photographs for the paper.

His first reviews were impressive. A critic for *Moving Picture World* wrote:

"The clever player who takes the role of the nervy and very nifty sharper in this picture is a comedian of the first water, who acts like one of Nature's own naturals. It is so full of action that it is indescribable, but so much of it is fresh and unexpected fun that a laugh will be going all the time almost. It is foolish-funny stuff that will make even the sober-minded laugh, but people out for an evening's good time will howl."

Mack Sennett knew he had found some special kind of comedian in Charlie Chaplin. He wasn't as enthusiastic as Chaplin about Charlie's approach to humor, but he recognized Chaplin's ability to make people laugh. He encouraged Charlie and helped Charlie gain confidence in his ideas. Sennett knew that audiences everywhere were beginning to take to Chaplin like they had never taken to any comedian before.

A week after Charlie's first comedy was ready for release to theaters, a second one was completed and distributed. It was called *The Kid Auto Races at Venice.*

For this film, Charlie dressed as the Tramp —baggy pants, tight coat, thin black string tie, black derby, big floppy shoes, flexible cane, and the small black mustache.

Charlie had learned enough from vaudeville to play his Tramp as a fellow who moves with ease, sometimes strutting, sometimes falling, always able to place a kick in the seat of the pants if needed. His Tramp was funny, but not yet as tender and as human as Charlie would later make him.

After six months of making a comedy every week or two, Charlie managed to turn out one that has stood the test of time as a genuine comic classic. It was *Tillie's Punctured Romance,* made with two gifted comediennes, Marie Dressler and Mabel Normand. Charlie plays a city slicker who gets Tillie to steal her father's savings and run away with him. Lots of funny situations and a hilarious chase by the famous Keystone Cops added up to a big hit at the box office and high critical acclaim. As George Blaisdell wrote in *Moving Picture World:*

"Chaplin outdoes Chaplin; that's all there is to it. His marvelous right-footed skid is just as funny in the last reel as it is in the first . . . ."

Charlie Chaplin's fame spread quickly. Even in those troubled years, when the world was entering World War I, audiences found Chaplin's humor and humanity too funny not to laugh at. As dozens of short comedies were made with Charlie in the next weeks and months, people all over the world started to recognize, laugh at, and love "the little fellow."

In English-speaking countries, captions for Chaplin's silent comedies would identify him as "Charlie." In other countries, audiences knew him as "Carlos," "Charlot," or "Carlito," and all laughed equally hard at him.

Within two years, girls in the Ziegfeld Follies were dancing to a routine about the Tramp, and Charlie Chaplin toys and dolls were sold by the tens of thousands. People stood in long lines at theaters to see his comedies. And soldiers sang songs about him as they marched off to war. Even children made up rhymes about him: "Charlie Chaplin went to France, to teach the ladies how to dance." While playing counting games, they'd chant: "Charlie Chaplin sat on a pin. How many inches did it go in?"

Puerto Rican children had a song all their own about Charlie, warning boys and girls who had a kitten to keep it indoors, because "Chali Chaplin" would come by and swat the kitten with his cane.

But Charlie didn't realize how much people loved him until he made a cross-country train ride from Hollywood to New York in 1916. Telegraph operators along the route tapped out the news: "Charlie Chaplin's train is stopping in your town!" Hundreds of people rushed to the train stations to see their new idol—the funniest man in the world. Charlie was thrilled, excited, and embarrassed by all the attention.

Charlie Chaplin at a Liberty Loan Rally in 1917.

Before he finished his third year in movies, Chaplin was earning $10,000 a week. And he was only 27 years old. Very soon, he would become a millionaire. And when the world's leading citizens came to the United States, they would make special trips to California to meet him and ask for his autograph.

In 1917, Charlie married a very pretty young lady named Mildred Harris. She wanted to be an actress. But neither their marriage nor her career worked out. They were divorced a few years later.

Charlie kept busy making movies, but he also helped in the war effort. He was one of the most successful show business salesmen for Liberty and War Bonds. But perhaps his greatest contribution to the war effort was his hilarious comedy about army life, *Shoulder Arms*.

When the movie came out in 1918, a critic for the *Chicago Herald* wrote:

"*Shoulder Arms* is very, very funny. Mr. Chaplin, with his sad seriousness, makes a delicious doughboy (soldier) and gets into situations amazing even for him. Laughter follows on his every moment and loud applause when he bags the person who is seeking safety in Holland (the Kaiser). And when he hates to get up in the morning—oh, me, we feel almost the sympathetic tear. It's a bravely jolly little picture, excellently done, and a concentration of brilliances, in a comedy way, like the light-shooting facets of a diamond."

But with fame came many problems. At first, Chaplin enjoyed the public adoration. But he soon began to wish he had some privacy. He couldn't go anywhere without being recognized and mobbed. And not all the critics adored him. Some thought that many things he did in his comedies were really rather tasteless and even vulgar. Others began complaining that Chaplin was earning as much money as the President of the United States. And some criticized him for marrying and divorcing so quickly.

In addition, Chaplin was having problems with his films. He overspent his movie budget. The producers would not help cover the expenses.

Some of Charlie's movie friends also were having problems with their studios. Almost by chance, they started their own movie-making company. Chaplin teamed with D. W. Griffith and two silent screen superstars, Mary Pickford and Douglas Fairbanks, in forming United Artists.

That year, Chaplin made his greatest movie thus far, *The Kid*. In the film, Chaplin played the Tramp. A child actor named Jackie Coogan played a poor boy of the streets, a role Charlie had lived himself as a hungry and lonely boy in London.

Moviegoers around the world fell under Chaplin's spell as never before. They also fell in love with the orphan boy he befriended. Critics lavished their highest praise:

"His new picture, *The Kid*, certainly outdoes in humor and the special brand of Chaplin pathos, anything this popular film star has yet produced," wrote a critic for *Theatre Magazine*. "There are almost as many tears as laughs in this movie—which proves the contention that Chaplin is almost as good a tragedian as he is a comedian. *The Kid* can be counted a screen masterpiece."

And so the movie has remained a masterpiece, often seen at Chaplin film festivals and on television among other classics of the silent screen.

Chaplin made only a few movies in the next four years. Two of the films used the Tramp character. Chaplin wrote, produced, and directed another of these films, *A Woman of Paris*. He appeared in it only briefly—a walk-on bit as a porter in a railroad station. The movie was more a drama than a comedy. It gave audiences and critics a chance to see what Chaplin could do with a different kind of film, one with a dramatic theme. But many people seemed to prefer Chaplin's comedies.

After *A Woman of Paris*, Chaplin made what many consider to be his greatest movie, *The Gold Rush*. This movie told about "the little fellow's" adventures in the Klondike. Chaplin proved that he could tell a long, and often serious, story, but still have the audiences howling in their seats.

Critics praised Chaplin and the movie:

"Here is a comedy with streaks of poetry, pathos, tenderness, linked with brusqueness and boisterousness," wrote Mordaunt Hall of *The New York Times*. "It is the outstanding gem of all Chaplin's pictures, as it has more thought and originality than even such masterpieces as *The Kid* and *Shoulder Arms*."

Harriette Underhill of *The New York Herald Tribune* added, "Praising one of Mr. Chaplin's pictures is like saying that Shakespeare is a good writer. And yet we heard people coming out of the theater after the performance was over saying, 'Do you know, I think Chaplin is a genius!' Well, so do we, but never has it been written so clearly in letters of fire as now."

Charlie Chaplin and Jackie Coogan in The Kid.

The Hero and Success

Chaplin's mother had recovered her health enough to come to America. The immigration authorities agreed to let her live in this country on a year-to-year permit. Charlie provided a home for her by the ocean, near his own estate in California, and found a nice couple to live with her. He also arranged for a nurse to take care of her. Charlie and Sydney visited her often. The family was together again.

But Charlie was tired and restless from his work. He couldn't seem to come up with an idea for another film. So he decided to go to Europe.

World War I had ended. Everywhere he went —London, Paris, Berlin—Charlie was hailed as a hero. Crowds swarmed around him. The rich and famous did their best to be invited to meet him.

When he returned from his European tour, he had a long talk with his mother. She told him that he was doing wonderfully in the movies, but she asked if he wouldn't rather be himself "than to live in the theatrical world of unreality?"

Chaplin laughed and told her that she was the one responsible for the unreality.

Hannah Chaplin didn't take offense at whatever Charlie meant by that. Instead she told him she was sorry he hadn't put his talent into becoming a preacher. Charlie said there wasn't much money in that.

It was three years before another Charlie Chaplin movie was completed and shown in theaters around the world. The film was *The Circus*. Hard as it was to follow *The Gold Rush* with a success, *The Circus* was acclaimed as another masterpiece. Again, Chaplin wrote, produced, directed, and starred in the movie.

Charlie played a circus performer in love with a beautiful bareback rider, whom he befriends. When she falls in love with a high-wire artist, Chaplin is heartbroken. But he helps the two find a happy life together in the circus, while he leaves the circus and their lives. The film is a mixture of humor and tragedy. One critic felt it might be "Chaplin's very greatest picture."

While Chaplin was making *The Circus*, he told his mother proudly that he was worth millions of dollars. Hannah Chaplin commented, "So long as you're able to keep your health and enjoy it."

Chaplin understood the wisdom of her words, but couldn't help but chuckle at it all. He remembered when they were poor; when Hannah could not meet the installment payments and her sewing machine had been taken away from her. With all his money, he could now buy his mother thousands of sewing machines if she wanted them.

Shortly afterward, Hannah Chaplin went to the hospital for surgery. Her heart was weak. Soon she went into a coma and died.

Chaplin had loved his mother always. He considered her a kind woman with many virtues, who did her best to raise her children and, when ill health came, took misfortune as cheerfully as she could. Even when they lived in poverty, Hannah Chaplin had maintained her dignity and taught her sons to work their way out of their condition.

Work was important to Charlie. He was happiest when he was working. He had a lot inside him that he still wanted to express. Making movies was the best way he knew to bring it out.

But movies were changing. In 1927, sound came to the screen, and a revolution hit the country. The public loved movies that had the sounds of running machines, laughter, singing, and talking. Overnight, silent movies were a thing of the past—as old-fashioned as the horse and buggy. By 1931, no producer would dream of making a silent movie.

Except one.

Charlie Chaplin was not convinced that sound movies were the only ones the public would go to see. And he wasn't sure he would be as funny if he talked. He considered himself primarily a mime. He had a big following as a silent comedian. Would the public like him if he spoke? Many other top stars flopped in their first talking pictures. Their voices just didn't match with what moviegoers thought they would sound like. Overnight, long and great careers were ended. Chaplin worried that his might end just as abruptly, if he spoke.

Charlie hadn't made a movie since The Circus. Now he set to work on what he considered to be his most ambitious movie so far, City Lights.

In the film, he is "the little fellow" again, this time in a big city, being bounced around by its impersonal, modern ways. He falls in love with a beautiful but blind flowergirl. He steals money so she can have an operation to restore her sight. She regains her sight, but he goes to prison for his crime. When he gets out, he meets the girl again. She thinks he's a tramp. In the end, she realizes that she owes her sight to him.

Audiences—by now used to talking pictures —found Chaplin's movie funny, touching, and beautiful. Critics praised it as one of Chaplin's best, and a few went so far as to call this film his greatest.

"Silence," said one critic, "if it's Chaplin who's silent—is still golden."

Charlie again returned to London for a visit. Again he was hailed as a hero. He traveled throughout Europe. Then he went to the Orient. Everywhere he went, thousands of people turned out to cheer the Tramp they loved.

Chaplin did not make another picture for five years. He was afraid to make a sound movie. Would audiences still laugh at him if he talked? Or would they laugh him off the sound screen?

Finally, in 1936, Charlie began work on *Modern Times*. It was supposed to be a sound movie, but at the last minute, Charlie decided to go completely against modern times and make another silent film. All his friends and associates tried to talk him out of it. But Chaplin was convinced that the public would still go to see a silent movie—if it was best to film the story without spoken dialogue.

Chaplin was right again. Audiences loved the movie, and critics hailed it as another classic.

Chaplin directing one of his films.

In a way, *Modern Times* marked a turning point in Chaplin's career.

Modern Times was Chaplin's first real attempt at social comment. He poked fun at big business. He showed what little chance the Tramp had with factory machines. Moviegoers and critics didn't pay much attention to any social message Chaplin was trying to get across to them. They were too busy laughing.

"Sociological concept?" wrote Frank S. Nugent of *The New York Times*. "Maybe. But a rousing, rib-tickling, gag-bestrewn jest for all that and in the best Chaplin manner. This morning there is good news. Chaplin is back again."

Chaplin married his leading lady from *Modern Times*, the young and beautiful Paulette Goddard. He said the bond between them was loneliness. Paulette had come to Hollywood from New York and knew no one. They dated and fell in love. After completing *Modern Times*, Chaplin suggested that they take a boat and go to China. Paulette said that she would love to go, but didn't have any clothes. Charlie said she could buy all she wanted in Honolulu. They were married and went on their way to China.

When they returned to Hollywood, Charlie again faced the old question of whether his next movie could be a silent film. By now it was 1940. Film audiences were used to talking pictures. Even Chaplin doubted that he could be a success in another silent film.

His worry worked a hardship on Paulette and his marriage. Eventually they were divorced. But Paulette found a lot of work as an actress. While Paulette was busy making movies, Charlie retreated to an oceanside cottage.

These were hard times in America. The nation was just starting to come out of its longest depression. Millions of people had been out of work. A drought had turned the middle of the United States into a huge dust bowl. All over the world, conditions were as bad or worse. And Europe seemed headed toward war. Some people thought that it might be a good thing for everyone if there was another world war. It could mean a lot of jobs for people out of work. Money could be made on the production of war goods.

Chaplin could not understand how these people could forget the terrible experiences of World War I. He couldn't imagine how the world would let itself get into another war.

He had trouble thinking of his next movie project. The possibility of war was on his mind. But then an old idea for a movie began nagging him. A British film producer, Alexander Korda, had suggested a story to him in 1937. He said that Chaplin should make a satire about Adolf Hitler involving mistaken identities. The Tramp could be mistaken for Hitler, because both wore the same small square black mustache.

Chaplin had not thought much of the idea when Korda first suggested it. But since then, Hitler's armies had been on the march, turning Europe into one big battleground. Chaplin was deeply troubled about the many people killed and injured in battle, and those made homeless and poor.

So he decided that he *would* make his next movie about Hitler. He would write it for humor but would try to get across some serious messages to the public. He would warn them not to let Hitler get any more powerful in Europe than he already was. He would play Hitler, whom he would call Hynkel in his movie. And he would also play Hynkel's look-alike, a barber. The barber would poke fun at Hynkel and later masquerade as him.

This appealed to Chaplin for his first sound movie, because he was afraid to give his classic character, the Tramp, a voice. He couldn't imagine what kind of voice it should be.

Chaplin called his movie *The Great Dictator*. This film, too, was a turning point for Chaplin.

It took Chaplin about two years to make *The Great Dictator*. After the first year, Chaplin ran into some censorship problems. England was not yet at war with Germany, and was cautious about creating any ill will with Hitler. The English were uncertain whether they could show the film. American movie censors also warned Chaplin that he should expect trouble if he was too outspoken in satirizing the Nazis or Hitler.

While making the anti-Nazi comedy, Chaplin got his first "hate" mail. He got letters from individuals and organizations warning him to stop the project. They said the movie never would be allowed to be shown in either America or England. Some people even threatened to throw stink bombs into the theaters and riot or shoot at the screen if the movie was released.

But Chaplin was more determined than ever to complete the picture. He said that he would rent his own halls to show the movie if he couldn't get it into theaters.

Before the movie was finished, England had declared war on Germany. Chaplin was vacationing on his boat off Catalina Island when he heard the news on the radio. He was happier than ever that he had decided to make the movie, and was eager to finish it.

Soon Chaplin was getting urgent telegrams from New York, impatiently asking for copies of the movie. Everyone who had heard of Chaplin's new film wanted desperately to see it.

Hitler had decided to invade Russia. Many people now *believed* what they had *feared*—that Hitler's ambitions for power had driven him mad. The United States had not yet entered the war, but many were concerned that there would be no way of staying out of it.

Controversy

When *The Great Dictator* was previewed in
New York late in 1940, the chief adviser to President Franklin D. Roosevelt was present. He told
Chaplin that it was a great movie, and a worth-
while film to make. But, he added, it would lose
money. Chaplin had spent $2 million and more
than two years working on the picture. He was
worried that it might flop.

The Great Dictator opened in New York
shortly afterward, and the public loved it. The
picture turned out to be the biggest money-maker
Chaplin had made up to that time. In that way,
the film was very successful.

Critics, however, gave the movie mixed reviews. Chaplin hadn't made a film in four years.
The critics expected a picture with the old Chaplin in it, hoping for the Tramp in his more usual
comedy role. What they saw was funny, but it
was a new Chaplin—the Chaplin with a message.
They had trouble accepting their old favorite in
the character of the world-conqueror Hynkel.

What bothered critics most was the final scene,
which was a strong speech denouncing dictators.

Chaplin as Hynkel in The Great Dictator.

America was not yet in the war. Many people squirmed uncomfortably in their movie seats when they heard Chaplin urging men and women everywhere to unite against the dictator who was enslaving Europe. It could mean only one thing to them: Chaplin was saying that the United States should declare war on Germany. *That* did not appeal to a great many people.

However, while older audiences felt a little uncomfortable with some of the film, younger audiences loved it all. Young Reviewers of the National Board of Review—made up of boys and girls aged 9 to 15—thought the picture was excellent. They especially liked Chaplin's final speech. One boy aged 9 wrote: "His speech tells us to be kind to everyone." Another boy, 13, wrote: "I liked the picture because it was down to earth and it shows the suffering of the people in Europe, and it shows Charlie Chaplin's true character." Perhaps that young reviewer came closer to the truth than any of the older critics.

Hollywood, too, recognized the genius of Chaplin in the movie. *The Great Dictator* was nominated for an Academy Award as best picture of the year, and Chaplin was nominated for best actor.

Amid all this, the Japanese attacked Pearl Harbor and the United States declared war on Japan, Germany's ally. Meanwhile, Hitler's armies had entered Russia. Hundreds of thousands of Russian civilians were bombed out of their homes and were starving in Moscow while the Nazis held the city under siege.

Chaplin got a telephone call now that was to change his life.

The Villain

The head of the American Committee for Russian War Relief called Charlie Chaplin and asked if he would speak at a rally in San Francisco. The rally was being held to raise money for starving Russian civilians. Chaplin was to "fill in" for the ambassador to Russia, Joseph E. Davies, who had come down with laryngitis. Chaplin accepted the invitation. In so doing, he began a chain of events that finally led to his exile from the United States.

Chaplin spoke in sympathy for the Russian cause, but stated that he was not a Communist. In those days, it was a very dangerous and unpopular thing to be even remotely connected with Communism.

"I am a human being," Chaplin told the rally, "and I think I know the reactions of human beings . . . . And at this moment Russian mothers are doing a lot of weeping and their sons a lot of dying . . . ."

The audience cheered him on. Perhaps they shouldn't have encouraged him so much. After all, he *was* an actor! And this *was* a "live" audience!

He spoke boldly to the audience. He urged them to give money for Russian War Relief. He ended his speech by urging President Roosevelt to support the Russians.

His speech meant that he wanted the United States to enter the war in Europe; to help with soldiers and arms. Some cheered him. Others now called him a Communist.

After the rally, a young actor had dinner with Chaplin. "You have a lot of courage," he told Charlie. Chaplin replied that he had only said what he sincerely felt, and what he thought was right.

But he began to worry. Had he let his principles run away with his tongue? Had he let the audience excite him with its cheering? Had he been carried away into saying something he would later regret? No, he decided he meant everything he said at the rally and would stand by it, for good or bad.

Several weeks later, Chaplin received another request. This time he was asked to speak at a mass rally of union workers at Madison Square Garden in New York. Chaplin accepted. For almost 15 minutes, a huge crowd listened to Chaplin talk to them by telephone from Hollywood! Again he urged relief for the Russian civilians. Again he urged the United States to send troops to help end the war. The crowd of 60,000 seemed to agree with Chaplin.

Then Chaplin was asked to speak at yet another New York rally. Friends advised him not to go, but he felt it would be a challenge. Chaplin liked challenge, so he went.

Many important people were to speak at the rally held on behalf of Russian War Relief. Since the Russians then were our allies, or friends, no one saw any harm in supporting a drive for food

Chaplin holding a Russian War Relief poster.

and clothing for the civilian victims of the war. But most of the other speakers were cautious in asking that the United States send soldiers to help Russia. Chaplin was determined to speak his mind about this topic, and he did.

A pro-Communist newspaper, the *Daily Worker*, reported the next day that the rally had been "a love feast between Charlie and the audience." Most other newspaper reports were less favorable. Again Chaplin was called a Communist, willing to sacrifice the lives of American soldiers in order to help the Russians drive off the Nazis.

After this rally, Chaplin noticed that he no longer was invited to his friends' homes. Charlie was deeply hurt. Because of his outspoken nature, he had lost not only the love of many movie fans, much of the press, and many critics, but also the few friends he had left.

He questioned his own motives in making the speeches. Was he just letting the cheering crowds stampede him into saying what they wanted to hear? Would he have taken up the anti-Nazi cause if he hadn't made a movie about it that cost him more than $2 million? Did he want to justify the movie and its cause? Was he just basically angry that his first talking picture was bringing him such grief? Or did he really believe the speeches he was making?

He decided that all of these things were true to some extent, but that he did believe wholeheartedly in the humanitarian things he was saying. He felt, like many others, that the United States would have to enter the war in Europe. The sooner it did, the shorter the war would be, and fewer soldiers and civilians would die.

Bad Times

Chaplin returned to California and began work on his next film. He went to meet an actress suggested for the role of leading lady in his movie. At last someone very pleasant entered Charlie's troubled life. He met Oona O'Neill, the daughter of one of America's greatest playwrights, Eugene O'Neill.

Although Chaplin never made the film, and never used Oona in any of his films, he was truly happy to be with her, to talk with her. In a short time they fell in love and decided to marry.

When they married, Chaplin was 54, Oona was 18. His critics, already calling him a Communist, now thought it was improper of him to marry someone so young.

Chaplin ignored his critics as best he could and tried not to make audiences and critics dislike him any more than they already did. Comedians were supposed to be funny, he knew, not controversial.

Instead he turned his energy to a new film he had written, *Monsieur Verdoux*. As many people and critics failed to understand his speeches on behalf of Russian War Relief, neither did they get Chaplin's message in *Monsieur Verdoux*. This film was about a murderer who seemed to make fun of his crimes. Chaplin tried to express in *Monsieur Verdoux* how he felt about the world war and the mass killing in war. But many people missed that message. They thought Chaplin was a Communist.

In 1947, 19 Hollywood people—actors, writers, directors, and others—were called to appear before the US Senate Committee on Un-American Activities. Chaplin was among the 19. He was to be questioned on whether or not he was a Communist.

The Committee's chairman was Senator Joseph McCarthy, who gained a reputation for trying to find Communists in the United States. Unfortunately, Senator McCarthy and his Committee used some bad methods. Sometimes innocent people lost their jobs and careers because the Committee branded them Communists. Sometimes these people really were not Communists, but just citizens who believed in freedom of speech and the right to help their less fortunate neighbors in the world. Many people feel that Chaplin was one of those whom McCarthy and the Committee persecuted and unjustly ruined.

Some of those questioned before the McCarthy Committee refused to say whether they were Communists. They felt that it was an infringement of their constitutional rights even to be asked the question. But Chaplin chose to speak out when he was asked whether or not he was a Communist. He sent the Committee a telegram that said in part: "I am not a Communist, neither have I ever joined any political party or organization in my life. I am what you call a 'peacemonger' . . . . " The Committee was satisfied, but Chaplin's critics were not.

The Chaplin family arriving in London in 1964
—(from left) Oona, Eugene, Chaplin, Victoria, Jane,

and Josephine. Annette, Michael, and Geraldine
are not in the picture.

Bittersweet Days

It was time, Chaplin felt, to turn away from controversy. He would make a non-political movie. He hoped to restore his lost popularity.

He spent the next four years making *Limelight*, a story about an aging music hall comedian in London. He would play the comedian, who was near death. His last months would be made happy by helping a young dancer restore her faith in herself and in life. The story was meant to encourage people everywhere, in the troubled years after the war, to have faith in themselves and in life.

The public loved the film. Some critics hailed it as another masterpiece. It wasn't the Chaplin they had known in earlier, happier days as the Tramp. As one critic put it: "Chaplin has captured the quality of longing, and nothing else matters."

After *Limelight* was finished, the Chaplins decided to go to England. Charlie wanted to show his family the city in which he was born. His wife wanted the children to go to school in Europe. She especially wanted them away from Hollywood.

Since Chaplin was still a British citizen, he had to apply for a permit to re-enter the United States. He did this months before they planned to leave. It wasn't until after Chaplin applied for his permit that he fully began to realize how unpopular he was with some Americans.

The government investigated Chaplin's political and private life. They looked into his tax records. But finally he was granted the permit to re-enter the country after his trip abroad. Immigration authorities even gave him a friendly pat on the back and wished him "bon voyage."

The Chaplins sailed toward England aboard the *Queen Elizabeth*. After only one day out on the Atlantic, Chaplin received a cable. It said he was barred from re-entering the United States. Before he could return to America, he would have to answer charges once again about both his political beliefs and his personal conduct. He was to do this before an Immigration Department Board of Inquiry.

It was the last straw for Chaplin. He was too tired, too weary, to go through these questions again.

They went on to England. In London, Chaplin was welcomed by a large crowd. He found that all over Europe, people still loved him. No one asked his politics or whether he was a Communist. He was loved for being himself, for bringing many hours of laughter, for being a "man of warmth."

Chaplin decided not to go back to America. The Chaplins settled in Europe to live and work.

Four years after leaving the United States, Chaplin made a movie called *A King in New York*, which he released in England in 1957. The film poked fun at just about every American sacred cow. Mouthwash, television, rock and roll music, big business. Although the movie had touches of the old Chaplin, there was not enough to please the public or critics. Many people thought they knew why Chaplin was poking fun at so much of American life. He was getting back at those who had smeared his name, who had forced him out of the United States.

Chaplin still lives in Europe, enjoying life with Oona and their eight children. He wrote, produced, and directed a film, *A Countess From Hong Kong,* in 1967. He also wrote the music for the film. Although the film had some funny moments, it was not a success.

60 *Charlie Chaplin accepting his Oscar from the Acad-*
emy of Motion Picture Arts and Sciences, 1972.

Epilogue

During his exile, Charlie Chaplin explained why he felt that he had made so many Americans angry with him: "My . . . sin was, and still is, being a nonconformist. Although I am not a Communist, I refused to fall in line by hating them. This, of course, has offended many . . . ."

He also felt that he was unpopular because he never became an American citizen. Many people thought he should have. But Chaplin argued that he paid his taxes to the United States. And he considered himself a "citizen of the world."

Being a citizen of the world—like so many of Chaplin's other concepts of individual freedom—was an idea ahead of its time. If he had made movies with strong social comments in the 1960s to mid-'70s, he probably would not have met with such criticism. Then, the United States had a more liberal climate.

In 1972, Chaplin was invited back to America. He was asked to appear at the Academy Awards ceremony in Los Angeles. He was to be given a special Oscar for the "humor and humanity" he brought to films for more than half a century.

Chaplin turned 83 in 1972. He surprised many people by attending the ceremony. He returned to the United States, the first time in over 20 years. And no one asked him for a return permit!

Accepting the Oscar—Chaplin's first major recognition from the movie industry he helped to become great—he had tears in his eyes. A standing ovation warmed his heart. To the audience and millions watching on television throughout the world, he said: "Words are so futile, so feeble, I can only say thank you for the honor of inviting me, all you wonderful, sweet people."

Without malice, "the little fellow" had come home.

Photo Credits

The Bettmann Archive, cover and pg. 4, pp. 20, 30, 39, 54-55; Culver Pictures, pp. 26, 34, 45, 49; Academy of Motion Picture Arts and Sciences, p. 60.